Introduction

Welcome to the London 2012 Olympic Games and Paralympic Games...

When the International Olympic Committee President Jacques Rogge announced in July 2005 that London had won the right to host the 2012 Games, the scenes of jubilation in Trafalgar Square were a clear indication of just what the Olympic Games and Paralympic Games meant to the people of the United Kingdom.

Fast-forward nearly seven years and the Games of the XXX Olympiad and the 14th Paralympic Games are now upon us.

If you thought those people in Trafalgar Square were excited, just wait till the greatest show on earth gets under way in July.

Yes, the Olympic Games and Paralympic Games remain the pinnacle of any athlete's career. They are the culmination of years of training, effort and dedication. They are events and experiences not to be missed, when the world comes together for four weeks of fun, festivities and friendship and when the ultimate competitors face the ultimate challenge...

The London 2012 Olympic Games
27 July – 12 August 2012

The London 2012 Paralympic Games
29 August – 9 September 2012

Meet the mascots

Here are Wenlock and Mandeville. You'll be seeing a lot of these two, as they are the London 2012 Games official mascots.

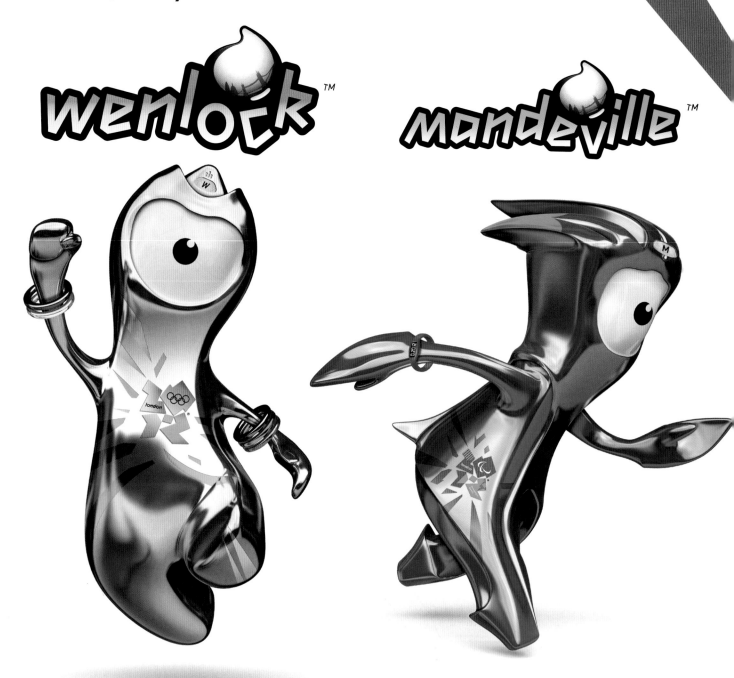

This is Wenlock, the official mascot for the London 2012 Olympic Games. He has been travelling around the United Kingdom, finding out about all of the fantastic Olympic Games sports involved and making a lot of friends along the way.

This is Mandeville, the official mascot for the London 2012 Paralympic Games. He is always ready for action and likes nothing better than having a go at something new.

1

Wenlock and Mandeville were created from two droplets of molten steel used to make the last girder for the Olympic Stadium.

2

Wenlock is named after Much Wenlock, the Shropshire town that once hosted a forerunner of the Olympic Games in 1850.

Five amazing London 2012 mascot facts

3

Mandeville, meanwhile, got his name from Stoke Mandeville, a Buckinghamshire hospital that used to organise the Stoke Mandeville Games, which were an inspiration for the Paralympic Games.

4

Wenlock has five friendship bracelets on his wrists, each representing one of the Olympic Rings, while the three points on his head represent the three places on the medal podium.

5

Mandevillle also has three points on his head – in red, blue and green – representing the *agitos*, the symbol of the Paralympic Games. He also wears a watch on his wrist with the time set to 0:20:12.

The history of the Olympic Games

It is now 116 years since the modern-day Olympic Games began and the competition – the experience – just keeps on getting better…

When the first modern Olympic Games were held in Athens in 1896 there were just 14 nations and a mere 241 competitors taking part. When the London 2012 Olympic Games begin in July, there will be an estimated 10,490 athletes representing some 200 countries, all giving everything in pursuit of Olympic Games glory.

The Games will celebrate their 116th birthday in 2012 and thanks to the spirit of everyone involved – the athletes, the officials, the fans and the International Olympic Committee – they have prospered, becoming the global phenomenon that they are today.

Of course, the Games wouldn't be the Games without the people everyone wants to see – the athletes. Over the years, there have been some truly memorable performances from some legendary competitors. Heroic and heart-wrenching, brave and beautiful, it's moments like these that have come to typify what the Olympic Games are all about…

George Eyser (USA)

Olympic Games: St Louis 1904

Sport: Gymnastics

Despite losing a leg in a train accident, American gymnast George Eyser nevertheless competed at the very highest level, winning six medals (three golds, two silvers and one bronze) in a single day at the St Louis 1904 Games.

Jim Thorpe (USA)

Olympic Games: Stockholm 1912

Sport: Athletics

One of the most versatile and naturally gifted athletes of all time, the USA's Jim Thorpe played professional baseball, basketball and American football in his career, but his crowning glory was taking two golds in the Pentathlon and the Decathlon in Stockholm.

The Olympic Games

Athens	1896	Tokyo	1964
Paris	1900	Mexico City	1968
St Louis	1904	Munich	1972
London	1908	Montreal	1976
Stockholm	1912	Moscow	1980
Antwerp	1920	Los Angeles	1984
Paris	1924	Seoul	1988
Amsterdam	1928	Barcelona	1992
Los Angeles	1932	Atlanta	1996
Berlin	1936	Sydney	2000
London	1948	Athens	2004
Helsinki	1952	Beijing	2008
Melbourne	1956	London	2012
Rome	1960		

Jesse Owens (USA)

Olympic Games: Berlin 1936

Sport: Athletics

The most successful athlete at the 1936 Games, Owens's astonishing performance in claiming gold medals in the 100m, 200m, Long Jump and 4 x 100m Relay distinguishes him as one of the great Olympians.

Fanny Blankers-Koen (The Netherlands)

Olympic Games: London 1948

Sport: Athletics

Nicknamed 'The Flying Housewife', Blankers-Koen was a 30-year-old mother of two from the Netherlands who many commentators suggested was too old to make an impression at London 1948. Gold medals in the 100m, 80m Hurdles, 200m and the 4 x 100m Relay proved otherwise.

Abebe Bikila (Ethiopia)

Olympic Games: Rome 1960, Tokyo 1964

Sport: Athletics

A last-minute addition to the Ethiopian team, Bikila didn't even have time to get a proper pair of running shoes for the Marathon in 1960 and chose to run barefoot instead. Four years later, he successfully defended his Marathon title at Tokyo 1964.

Bob Beamon (USA)

Olympic Games: Mexico City 1968

Sport: Athletics

America's Bob Beamon didn't just break the Long Jump world record when he took gold in Mexico City, he smashed it beyond all recognition with his leap of 8.90m, some 55cm longer than the previous best mark. It was a record that would stand for 23 years.

Mark Spitz (USA)

Olympic Games: Mexico City 1968, Munich 1972

Sport: Aquatics – Swimming

Some athletes dedicate their entire careers to the pursuit of just one Olympic gold medal but American swimmer Mark Spitz stunned the watching world by taking a record seven at Munich 1972.

Nadia Comaneci (Romania)

Olympic Games: Montreal 1976, Moscow 1980

Sport: Gymnastics

Winner of three gold medals in Gymnastics in 1976, the young Romanian's performance in Montreal made history as the first time a perfect score of 10 had ever been awarded. The feat was so rare that the scoreboards were not even able to display a score of 10.0, showing it as 1.00 instead!

Steve Redgrave (Great Britain)

Olympic Games: Los Angeles 1984, Seoul 1988, Barcelona 1992, Atlanta 1996, Sydney 2000

Sport: Rowing

Starting in 1984 and over the course of 16 years and five different Olympic Games, Great Britain's Steve Redgrave's superhuman strength saw him claim an unprecedented five gold medals in Rowing. It also earned him a knighthood from Her Majesty the Queen.

Michael Johnson (USA)

Olympic Games: Barcelona 1992, Atlanta 1996, Sydney 2000

Sport: Athletics

His upright running style may have been unorthodox but there was no doubting the natural talent of USA's Michael Johnson. The 200m world record time of 19.32 he set in the Atlanta 1996 Games was a mark that would stand for 12 years.

Pyrros Dimas (Greece)

Olympic Games: Barcelona 1992, Atlanta 1996, Sydney 2000, Athens 2004

Sport: Weightlifting

A legend in the world of Weightlifting, Pyrros Dimas won gold at the Games in 1992, 1996 and 2000 and even took a bronze when injured during the Games in Athens in 2004. After winning the bronze he announced his retirement by leaving his shoes on the stage as applause rang out across the arena.

Usain Bolt (Jamaica)

Olympic Games: Beijing 2008

Sport: Athletics

Everybody knew that Jamaica's Usain Bolt was quick but nobody really expected the record books to be rewritten in such a staggering manner. After smashing the 100m world record (and slowing down in the last 10 metres), he then beat the 200m world record too before going on to win the 4 x 100m Relay with the Jamaican team in another world record time.

Chris Hoy (Great Britain)

Olympic Games: Sydney 2000, Athens 20004, Beijing 2008

Sport: Cycling – Track

Chris Hoy's triple gold success on the cycle track at Beijing 2008 proved to be the catalyst for a huge upsurge in interest in Cycling in the United Kingdom. Like Steve Redgrave's, Hoy's efforts were also rewarded with a knighthood.

The history of the Paralympic Games

The Paralympic Games have a habit of making heroes. Here, then, is just a small selection of the living legends who have made their name at Paralympic Games gone by...

The Paralympic Games have come a very long way since their humble beginnings as the 1948 Stoke Mandeville Games, a sporting competition for servicemen injured in World War II. Over the years that followed the idea of an international event for disabled athletes gathered pace until 1960, when the first official Paralympic Games were held in Rome, with approximately 400 athletes from 23 countries participating. By 1976, those numbers had been bolstered to more than 1,600 competitors from 40 countries, thanks largely to the inclusion of more disability classifications, and by 1988 in Seoul, South Korea, the Paralympic Games were now taking place in the same city as the Olympic Games themselves. Today, of course, the Paralympic Games are firmly established as one of the world's biggest and most watched sporting events. Indeed, they have grown, prospered and developed into a sporting spectacle unlike any other, where competitors from the world over push their bodies to the limit and defy the odds in their pursuit of Paralympic glory. Put simply, it is sport at its purest.

Trischa Zorn (USA)

Paralympic Games: Arnhem 1980, New York City 1984, Seoul 1988, Barcelona 1992, Atlanta 1996, Sydney 2000, Athens 2004

Sport: Swimming

Blind since birth, USA swimmer Trischa Zorn has won more medals than any other Paralympic athlete in history and her total of 46 medals spread over seven different Games is a record unlikely to be beaten.

Tanni Grey Thompson (Great Britain)

Paralympic Games: Seoul 1988, Barcelona 1992, Atlanta 1996, Sydney 2000, Athens 2004

Sport: Athletics

Tanni Grey-Thompson, or Baroness Grey-Thompson to give her her full title, is one of Great Britain's greatest ever Paralympians. With 16 Paralympic medals to her name – including 11 golds – she has also set 35 world records on the Athletics track. Her legendary status assured, she retired from competition in 2007.

The Paralympic Games

Rome	1960	Seoul	1988
Tokyo	1964	Barcelona	1992
Tel Aviv	1968	Atlanta	1996
Heidelberg	1972	Sydney	2000
Toronto	1976	Athens	2004
Arnhem	1980	Beijing	2008
New York City and		London	2012
Stoke Mandeville	1984		

Esther Vergeer (Netherlands)

Paralympic Games: Sydney 2000, Athens 2004, Beijing 2008

Sport: Wheelchair Tennis

This Dutch Wheelchair Tennis player is one of the all-time greats of the game. She has won over 400 consecutive matches (she's not lost a singles game since January 2003) and as well as 19 Grand Slam titles she also has five Paralympic gold medals.

Franz Nietlispach (Switzerland)

Paralympic Games: Toronto 1976, Arnhem 1980, New York City 1984, Seoul 1988, Barcelona 1992, Atlanta 1996, Sydney 2000, Athens 2004, Beijing 2008

Sports: Athletics, Table Tennis and Cycling – Road

A legend of the Paralympic Games, Nietlispach won an incredible 14 gold, six silver and one bronze in Athletics between 1980 and 2000 as well as representing Switzerland at Table Tennis in the 1976 and 1980 Games. Not content with that, he then went and won a bronze in Track Cycling at the 2004 Games in Athens.

Dervis Konuralp (Great Britain)

Paralympic Games: Atlanta 1996, Sydney 2000, Athens 2004, Beijing 2008

Sport: Swimming

A London 2012 Olympic and Paralympic ambassador, Konuralp learned to swim at primary school when his visual impairment worsened. His progress was nothing short of phenomenal. By the age of 15 he was representing Great Britain at the Paralympic Games of Atlanta 1996 and at 17 he was a world champion and world record holder. He has competed in a further three Paralympic Games.

They said it!

It's often difficult for athletes to put into words just what the Olympic Games and Paralympic Games mean to them. But these guys certainly did a pretty good job...

'For athletes, the Olympics are the ultimate test of their worth.'

Mary Lou Retton, USA gold medal-winning gymnast from the Los Angeles 1984 Olympic Games.

'An Olympic medal is the greatest achievement and honour that can be received by an athlete. I would swap any world title to have won gold at the Olympics.'

Australian boxer Jeff Fenech, who competed in the 1984 Olympic Games in Los Angeles.

'The Olympics remain the most compelling search for excellence that exists in sport, and maybe in life itself.'

Dawn Fraser, Australian swimmer and gold medallist at the 1956, 1960 and 1964 Olympic Games.

'A loser is not the one who runs last in the race, but the one who sits and watches and has never tried to run.'

South African athlete Oscar Pistorius offers some inspirational words ahead of the the London 2012 Games.

'When you cross the line, it is such a wonderful feeling it's hard to describe.'

Great Britain's Kelly Holmes, two-time Olympic gold medallist at the Athens 2004 Olympic Games.

'My goal is one Olympic gold medal. Not many people in this world can say, "I'm an Olympic gold medallist."'

Michael Phelps, the USA swimmer who has won a remarkable 14 gold medals at the Olympic Games.

'I think when you have a disability people are always putting limitations on you, telling you, even in a nice way, what you can't do. My attitude to that has always been: You can't tell me that. I'll show you.'

Louise Sauvage, Australia's nine-time gold medallist in Athletics.

'I get nervous but that drives you on and makes you want to do well.'

Great Britain's Paralympic Swimming gold medallist Ellie Simmonds.

'A lifetime of training for just ten seconds.'

USA sprinter Jesse Owens, winner of four gold medals at the Berlin 1936 Olympic Games.

'It is the inspiration of the Olympic Games that drives people not only to compete but to improve, and to bring lasting spiritual and moral benefits to the athlete and inspiration to those lucky enough to witness the athletic dedication.'

Herb Elliott, Australian middle-distance runner and 1500m gold medal winner at the Rome 1960 Olympic Games.

The London 2012 Games venues...

From new venues like the Olympic Stadium, Velodrome and the Aquatics Centre to iconic venues like Wembley Stadium and The Royal Artillery Barracks, the London 2012 Games competitors will have only the greatest arenas and the finest facilities in which to perform. Here is a selection of some of the amazing London 2012 venues...

Olympic Stadium

As the signature venue of London 2012, the Olympic Stadium certainly doesn't disappoint. Spectators will reach the venue via five bridges that link the site to the surrounding area while inside there are 25,000 seats in its permanent lower tier and a lightweight steel and concrete upper tier holding a further 50,000 spectators.

Did you know? The Olympic Stadium has around 700 rooms, including changing rooms and toilets.
Events: Opening and Closing Ceremonies, Athletics and Paralympic Athletics

ExCeL

In the shadow of City Airport in London's Docklands, ExCeL's position as one of the capital's largest exhibition centres makes it ideal for hosting a wide variety of sports. For London 2012 it will be divided into five separate arenas.

Did you know? Since 2000, ExCeL has entertained more than 5 million visitors from over 200 countries.
Sports: Boxing, Fencing, Judo, Table Tennis, Taekwondo, Weightlifting, Wrestling, Boccia, Paralympic Table Tennis, Paralympic Judo, Powerlifting, Sitting Volleyball, Wheelchair Fencing

Aquatics Centre

Located in the south-east corner of the Olympic Park, the new Aquatics Centre was designed by acclaimed international architect Zaha Hadid and features a spectacular wave-like roof that is 160m long and up to 80m wide. Inside there is a 50m competition pool, a 25m competition diving pool, a 50m warm-up pool and a 'dry' warm-up area for divers.

Did you know? The roof of the centre has a longer single span than Heathrow Airport's Terminal 5.
Sports: Diving, Modern Pentathlon (swimming), Paralympic Swimming, Swimming, Synchronised Swimming

Water Polo Arena

This spectacular new wedge-shaped arena has been designed to complement the look of the neighbouring Aquatics Centre and features a distinctive roof that rises from 12m high on one side up to 25m on the other.

Did you know? The arena's roof is made of recycled PVC cushions inflated with air to provide extra insulation.
Sports: Water Polo

Velodrome

This stunning new venue was the first Olympic venue to be completed and boasts a state-of-the-art track made from sustainably sourced Siberian Pine and a glass window between its two tiers offering a panoramic 360-degree view of the Olympic Park.

Did you know? Great Britain's Olympic Cycling champion Sir Chris Hoy was involved in the design consultation for the Velodrome.
Sports: Track Cycling, Paralympic Track Cycling

The Royal Artillery Barracks

The historic 18th-century Royal Artillery Barracks will provide the perfect backdrop for the Shooting events. For the Games there will be four temporary indoor ranges built for Pistol and Rifle Shooting, with outdoor ranges for the Trap and Skeet events.

Did you know? The Royal Artillery Barracks have the longest continuous façade of any building in the United Kingdom.
Sports: Shooting, Paralympic Archery, Paralympic Shooting

North Greenwich Arena

The former Millennium Dome has been transformed into a spectacular venue capable of hosting a variety of events. Today, it is rightly regarded as one of the best venues in the world, attracting the biggest names in entertainment and sport. Perfect, then, for hosting some Games events.

Did you know? If you laid the Eiffel Tower on its side it would still fit inside the North Greenwich Arena.
Sports: Gymnastics – Artistic, Gymnastics – Trampoline, Basketball, Wheelchair Basketball

Eton Dorney

Situated 40 kilometres west of London close to Windsor Castle, Eton Dorney is already used to host international rowing regattas as well as providing world-class training facilities. Opened in 2006, the main lake here is 2,200m long with eight lanes, each 13.5m wide, and with a minimum depth of 3.5m.

Did you know? The lake here was the idea of teachers from the famous Eton College, who wanted a still-water rowing course so they didn't have to brave the choppier waters of the River Thames.
Sports: Canoe Sprint, Rowing, Paralympic Rowing

Wembley Stadium

Redesigned, rebuilt and now boasting an iconic 130m-high arch, the new Wembley Stadium was opened in 2007 on the same site as the old Empire Stadium. While it may have changed its appearance, for many it remains the spiritual home of football. Some of the UK's biggest and best football stadia will also be used at London 2012, these are Hampden Park, the Millennium Stadium, Old Trafford, St James' Park and the City of Coventry Stadium.

Did You Know? Every seat at the new Wembley Stadium has more leg room than the seats in the Royal Box at the old Wembley.
Sports: Football

Lee Valley White Water Centre

Part of the 42-km-long, 4,000- hectare Lee Valley Regional Park in Hertfordshire, the Lee Valley White Water Centre is a new permanent facility made up of two courses – one for competition and another for training. After the Games, the centre will be open to the public as well as elite athletes.

Did you know? Fifteen cubic metres of water per second will flow into the 300m competition course – enough to fill a 50m swimming pool every minute.
Sports: Canoe Slalom

Know the Olympic Games sports

From Archery to Athletics, Taekwondo to Triathlon, there's something for everyone at London 2012. The only problem is trying to choose which sport to enjoy…

Aquatics

Staged in the state-of-the-art new Aquatics Centre, there's a wealth of wonderfully wet events to enjoy in the pool at London 2012, including Diving (eight events), Swimming (34 events), Synchronised Swimming (two events) and Water Polo (two events).

Badminton

There will be five gold medals up for grabs at Wembley Arena in Badminton, with Singles and Doubles for men and women and Mixed doubles. Matches are played as the best of three games, with each game played to 21 points.

Archery

Held in the historic setting of the home of cricket, Lord's, Archery features Individual and Team competitions for both men and women. There'll also be a new scoring system too, with archers scoring points in sets, much like volleyball.

Basketball

Twelve teams will compete in both the men's and the women's competitions. The group stage games and women's quarter-finals will be held in the White Hall in the Olympic Park before moving on to the 20,000-capacity North Greenwich Arena for the latter stages.

Athletics

From the track to the field and out on to the wide-open road, Athletics remains one of the most popular sports in the Olympic Games. At London 2012, there will be 47 different events to enjoy, including 42 at the Olympic Stadium.

Boxing

For the first time at an Olympic Games there will also be a women's competition, with three weight divisions offering medals. The men's competition, meanwhile, will have 10 weight divisions.

Canoeing

With the four Canoe Slalom events being hosted at the impressive new Lee Valley White Water Centre and the 12 Canoe Sprint events being held at Eton Dorney, Canoeing is shaping up to be one of the highlights of London 2012.

Cycling

The new 6,000-seater Velodrome will host the 10 Track Cycling events, while there's also another eight adrenalin-fuelled events in BMX, Mountain Bike and Road Cycling.

Equestrian

There are six gold medals up for grabs in Equestrian, with Individual and Team competitions in Dressage, Eventing and Jumping, all taking place at Greenwich Park.

Fencing

Fencing has featured at every Olympic Games of the modern era and at London 2012 ExCeL will host 10 events, including the Individual Epée, Individual Foil, Individual Sabre, Team Foil, Team Sabre and Team Epée.

Football

Some of the biggest and best stadia in the United Kingdom will host the 16 teams for men, 12 for women team tournaments in Football, including Old Trafford, City of Coventry, Hampden Park, the Millennium Stadium and, of course, Wembley Stadium.

Gymnastics

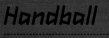

The North Greenwich Arena will stage 14 medal events in Artistic Gymnastics and two further events in Trampoline, while Wembley Arena will host the two medal events in Rhythmic Gymnastics.

Handball

Two 12-team events – men's and women's – will begin with the preliminaries and women's quarter-finals at the new Copper Box, before moving on to the White Hall for the men's quarter-finals, plus all semi-finals and finals.

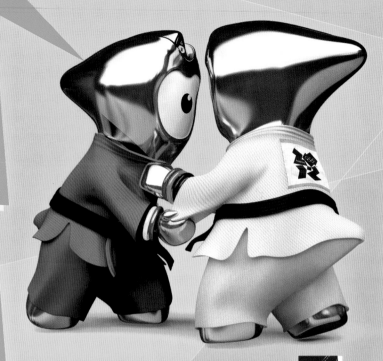

Hockey

As ever, this perennially popular sport will feature two 12-team tournaments, for men and women, with all the games taking place at the new Riverbank Arena at the Olympic Park.

Judo

Nearly 400 athletes will be lining up at ExCeL for Judo and with 14 medal events across 14 weight divisions on offer, there's going to be a lot of explosive action to take in.

Modern Pentathlon

The Modern Pentathlon will be celebrating 100 years of Olympic competition when it begins at London 2012. A sport like no other, competitors face five challenges: fencing, swimming, riding and the combined event (running and shooting).

Rowing

The ultimate test of strength and endurance, Rowing at London 2012 features eight men's events and six women's events, with the action taking place on the world-class course of Eton Dorney.

Sailing

A total of 380 sailors will decamp to Weymouth and Portland on the south coast of England to compete in 10 medal events over 14 action-packed days.

Shooting

Against the stunning backdrop of The Royal Artillery Barracks, Shooting will once more test the nerve and concentration of the world's best marksmen and women. There are 15 medal events using pistols, rifles and shotguns.

Table Tennis

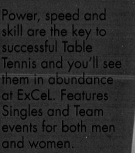

Power, speed and skill are the key to successful Table Tennis and you'll see them in abundance at ExCeL. Features Singles and Team events for both men and women.

Taekwondo

The Korean word *Taekwondo* translates as 'the way of foot and fist', which is the perfect description of this high-energy martial art. At London 2012 there will be four weight classes for both men and women, with eight medals up for grabs.

Weightlifting

Witness the closest thing to superhuman strength at the Olympic Weightlifting. At London 2012 there will be 15 medal events (eight men's and seven women's). Expect the unexpected.

Tennis

A little over three weeks after the end of the famous Wimbledon championships the cream of the world's tennis talent will be back in London SW19 in pursuit of the ultimate prize – Olympic gold. Medals will be awarded in Singles and Doubles for men and women and Mixed Doubles.

Triathlon

One of the fastest-growing sports in the world, the Triathlon demands exceptional levels of fitness and fortitude. Beginning and ending in London's Hyde Park, competitors face a 1500m swim, followed by a 40km bike ride and a gruelling 10km run to finish.

Wrestling

Divided into Freestyle Wrestling (where you can use all parts of the body) and Greco-Roman Wrestling (where you can only use arms and upper bodies), this sport requires strength, power and, crucially, technique. It features 18 medal events.

Volleyball

Fast, frenetic and fun, the indoor Volleyball is always a crowd favourite and at London 2012 there will be a 12-team tournament for both men and women. Beach Volleyball, meanwhile, takes place on Horse Guards Parade and consists of two 24-team tournaments for men and women.

21

Aquatics events

The wide range of Aquatics events at the London 2012 Olympic Games will mean there is incredible action in the pools...

Know the events

The Aquatics programme features four disciplines, namely Swimming, Synchronised Swimming, Diving and Water Polo. In the Swimming, there are four strokes (Freestyle, Backstroke, Breaststroke and Butterfly), with races from 50m up to 1500m and Individual Medley, Freestyle and Medley Relay events. There is also the 10km Marathon Swimming in open water. Synchronised Swimming, where competitors perform routines to music, takes place as either a Duet or a Team event, while Diving features four events for men and four for women, namely the 3m Springboard, the 10m Platform, the Synchronised 3m Springboard and the Synchronised 10m Platform. The men's Water Polo event, is contested by 12 teams, while the women's is contested by eight teams.

British swimmer Rebecca Adlington won two golds in Beijing 2008 and she will be a medal contender at London 2012.

Olympic Games history

Swimming has been an ever-present part of the story since the Olympic Games began in 1896, although in the early days the races tended to take place in open water. In Paris in 1900, for instance, the events took place in the River Seine. Synchronised Swimming, meanwhile, did not feature until the Los Angeles 1984 Olympic Games, while Diving first appeared in St Louis 1904 (when they also had a 'Plunge' event, which was, essentially, a long jump for divers). Water Polo debuted as a 12-team event at the 1920 Olympic Games in Antwerp, Belgium.

Great Britain's Henry Taylor wins the gold medal in the men's 1500m Freestyle Swimming at the London 1908 Olympic Games.

The lowdown

Swimming
Venue: Aquatics Centre – Olympic Park (pool events); Hyde Park (Marathon Swimming 10km)

Dates: Saturday 28 July – Saturday 4 August (Aquatics Centre); Thursday 9 – Friday 10 August (Hyde Park)

Medal events: 34

Synchronised Swimming
Venue: Aquatics Centre – Olympic Park

Dates: Sunday 5 – Friday 10 August

Medal events: 2

Diving
Venue: Aquatics Centre – Olympic Park

Dates: Sunday 29 July – Saturday 11 August 2012

Medal events: 8

Water Polo
Venue: Olympic Park – Water Polo Arena

Dates: Sunday 29 July – Sunday 12 August

Medal events: 2

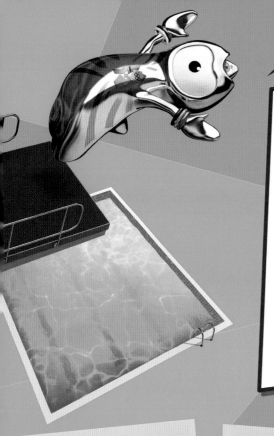

What they say

'In London, it will be an all-or-nothing approach... I'd rather take the risk because I'll only have this chance once in a lifetime to compete in front of a home crowd at an Olympics.'

Great Britain's teenage diving sensation Tom Daley.

Did you know?

Underwater Swimming featured at the Paris 1900 Olympic Games. Competitors earned points for the length of time they spent and distance they went underwater.

Amazing fact!

Synchronised Swimming actually began as a sport for men in the 1800s. Today, though, it is one of just two sports in the Olympic programme to be contested only by women, the other being Rhythmic Gymnastics.

One to watch

Tamás Kásás (Hungary)

This Hungarian water polo player is arguably the greatest defensive player of his generation. The linchpin of his national team, Kásás has won the gold medal in each of the last three Olympic Games in Sydney, Athens and Beijing.

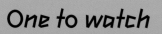

Athletics – track

Speed and endurance are the essential factors for being successful at the 24 Athletics track events...

Know the events

Staged in the spectacular new Olympic Stadium, the 24 track events (12 for men, 12 for women) will be held over distances ranging from 100m to 10,000m. There are five Road events too, including the men's and women's Marathon. The majority of track events will begin with one or more rounds of heats, with the best athletes eventually qualifying for the final. There are, of course, two combined events as well. The women's Heptathlon features seven track and field events (see page 25), while the men compete in the Decathlon, which features 10 events.

Olympic Games history

The ancient Olympic Games featured the 'stadium' race, a sprint of approximately 192 metres, and there's historical evidence to suggest that the race took place as long ago as 776 BC. The first modern Olympic Games in Athens in 1896 also included a Marathon as a link to ancient Greece. Twelve years later in London, the race's distance was extended from around 25 miles to 26.2 miles (42.195 kilometres) so that it finished in front of the Royal Box. This distance is still used today.

The lowdown

Venue: Olympic Stadium – Olympic Park (Athletics track); The Mall (Marathon and Race Walk)

Dates: Friday 3 August – Sunday 12 August

Medal events: 47

Did you know?

When Usain Bolt won the 100m at Beijing 2008, he not only did it in a new world record time but he also did it with his shoelace undone!

What they say

'London is the key. That is what matters... The aim is to get back to that world record time for next season. For London.'

Usain Bolt, Jamaica's sprint sensation and triple gold medal winner at Beijing 2008.

- ✪ 100m
- ✪ 200m
- ✪ 400m
- ✪ 4 x 100m Relay
- ✪ 4 x 400m Relay
- ✪ 100m, 110m and 400m Hurdles
- ✪ 800m
- ✪ 1500m
- ✪ 3000m Steeplechase
- ✪ 5000m
- ✪ 10,000m

Road events

- ✪ Marathon
- ✪ 20km and 50km Race Walk

One to watch

Kirani James (Grenada)

He may be only 19 years old, but Grenada's 400m runner Kirani James is the young man everyone is talking about. In his first ever professional race in London in August 2011, he blitzed the field, clocking an incredible time of 44.61.

Heptathlon / Decathlon

Featuring a mix of track and field events, the Heptathlon and Decathlon test an athlete's fitness and technique to the limit.

Know the events

The Heptathlon is contested by women and consists of seven events (100m hurdles, 200m, 800m, high jump, shot put, javelin throw and long jump), while the Decathlon sees men compete over 10 events (100m, 110m hurdles, 400m, 1500m, long jump, high jump, shot put, pole vault, discus throw and javelin throw).

Both events tend to see great camaraderie develop between athletes, with the winners generally recognised as the best all-round athletes in the competition.

Combined events

- ✪ Heptathlon
- ✪ Decathlon

Amazing fact!

There will be 510 adjustable hurdles used throughout the Athletics competition at London 2012.

Great Britain's Jessica Ennis will be one of the leading contenders in the London 2012 Heptathlon.

⍳ Athletics — field

Speed, technique and vast reserves of power – those are what you need to succeed in the Olympic Games Athletics field events...

Know the events

There are 16 field events at the Olympic Games, split between four jumping events (High Jump, Pole Vault, Long Jump and Triple Jump) and four throwing events (Shot Put, Discus Throw, Hammer Throw and Javelin Throw). All field events begin with a qualification stage, with the best athletes qualifying for the final.

Olympic Games history

Generally speaking, the throwing events have tended to be for men only, but over time women too have participated. The Hammer, for example, has been part of the Games since 1900 but the women's Hammer only made its Olympic Games debut at Sydney 2000, a full century later. It's a similar story with the jumping events. The Triple Jump was part of the very first modern Olympic Games in Athens in 1896, but it only became a women's medal event at Atlanta 1996. Today, men and women have the same roster of events.

The lowdown

Venue: Olympic Stadium – Olympic Park

Dates: Friday 3 August – Sunday 12 August

Medal events: 47

One to watch

Teddy Tamgho (France)

The 2010 European and World Indoor Triple Jump Champion, this young Frenchman could be the one who finally overhauls Jonathan Edwards's long-standing world record of 18.29m. With a personal best of 17.98m and with time on his side, he stands every chance. Expect a fascinating head-to-head with Great Britain's Phillips Idowu.

What they say

'A good career is a long-lasting career. When you're there in every competition doing a good job you're a part of an elite, and that's the most important thing.'

Blanka Vlašić, Croatian high jumper.

Did you know?

The design of the javelin was modified in the mid-1980s as throwers like Germany's Uwe Hohn were throwing it so far it was endangering spectators at the other end of the stadium.

Amazing fact!

The USA's Guinn Smith became the last pole vaulter to win a gold medal using a bamboo pole when he leapt to victory at the London 1948 Games.

List of events

- ✪ High Jump
- ✪ Pole Vault
- ✪ Long Jump
- ✪ Triple Jump
- ✪ Shot Put
- ✪ Discus Throw
- ✪ Hammer Throw
- ✪ Javelin Throw

Estonian discus thrower Gerd Kanter won the 2008 Olympic Games title with a throw of 68.82m.

Boxing

Power, speed, agility and timing – the Boxing events are everything that Olympic competition should be…

Know the events

The Olympic Boxing competition will feature 10 men's weight categories, from Light Fly Weight (46–49kg) to Super Heavy Weight (over 91kg). At London 2012, women's Boxing will also feature as a full Olympic medal event for the very first time, with medals in three weight divisions. Each class is run in a knockout format, with the winners of the two semi-finals fighting for the gold medal and the two losers each awarded a bronze. The bouts themselves, meanwhile, will take place over three three-minute rounds for men and four two-minute rounds for women.

Olympic Games history

Boxing made its first appearance in the Olympic Games in St Louis in 1904 and has been at every Games since, with the exception of Stockholm in 1912. It has proved to be a sport that creates more superstars than most, with the likes of Cassius Clay (later known as Muhammad Ali), George Foreman and Oscar de la Hoya all winning Olympic Games gold.

The lowdown

Venue: ExCeL

Dates: Saturday 28 July – Sunday 12 August

Medal events: 13

Did you know?

An Olympic Boxing glove weighs 284 grams.

Amazing fact!

During the London 2012 Olympic Games, the Boxing competitors will get through 432 pairs of gloves.

What they say

'**The pinnacle of boxing is the Olympic Games and that's what every boxer is aiming for.**'

Tom Stalker, captain of Great Britain's Boxing team.

One to watch

Nicola Adams (Great Britain)

The Leeds Fly Weight was the first British woman to win a major title when she won European gold in October 2011. Now 29, she's at the peak of her powers and is a contender for gold at London 2012. 'It's about making the most of it,' she says. 'There might not be another Olympics in our country in our lifetime, and I can't imagine what an amazing and exciting experience it is going to be.'

Canoeing

Held at the spectacular Lee Valley White Water Centre and the straights at Eton Dorney, the Olympic Canoeing is guaranteed to get you on the edge of your seat...

Know the events

The Canoeing programme is divided between the Canoe Slalom and Canoe Sprint events. In the Canoe Slalom, competitors use small, agile boats to navigate a white-water course with up to 25 gates, all against the clock. In the sprint, meanwhile, the boat is longer and more streamlined and races are held over 200m, 500m or 1000m, either solo, in pairs or in teams of four.

Olympic Games history

Canoe and kayak racing first became full medal sports at the Berlin 1936 Olympic Games, but Canoe Slalom didn't appear until Munich 1972 and became a permanent part of the Olympic programme in 1992. The first Canoe Sprint took place at the Paris 1924 Olympic Games as a demonstration sport and became a full Olympic Sport 12 years later in Berlin.

The lowdown

Canoe Slalom
Venue: Lee Valley White Water Centre

Dates: Sunday 29 July – Thursday 2 August

Medal events: 4

Canoe Sprint
Venue: Eton Dorney

Dates: Monday 6 – Saturday 11 August

Medal events: 12

Amazing fact!

A total of 200 gate poles need to be painted red and green for the Canoe Slalom course.

Did you know?

In its early days of competition, Canoe Slalom events were actually held on flat water before being switched to white-water rapids.

One to watch

Katalin Kovács (Hungary)

This Hungarian sprinter is a legend in the sport, having taking 38 medals at the World Championships (including 29 golds) and taken Olympic gold in the Kayak Double (K2) 500m event in the Athens 2004 Games and the Beijing 2008 Olympic Games. Expect a hat-trick at London 2012.

What they say

'White-water canoeing is such a difficult sport that you have to concentrate from beginning to end, because you can make a mistake down to the last second or in the last metre. Even the greatest favourites make mistakes and only once you have crossed the finishing line can you say, "OK, now I've made it".'

Michal Martikán, Slovakia's double gold medal winner.

Cycling

Where two wheels and 18 medal events mean more high-speed action than ever at London 2012...

Know the events

There are four disciplines across the sport of Cycling at London 2012, namely Track (10 medal events), Road (four events), Mountain Bike (two events) and BMX (two events). All Track events will take place at the spectacular new Velodrome in the Olympic Park, while the Road Races will be contested over a 250km course for men and a 140km course for women. The shorter Time Trials, meanwhile, will be held over 44km and 29km for men and women respectively. In the Mountain Bike event, races will take around one hour and 45 minutes over rough and hilly terrain, while the BMX races are held over a short, undulating track with each race taking around 40 seconds.

Great Britain's Shanaze Reade leads the race field in the women's BMX final at the Beijing 2008 Olympic Games.

Olympic Games history

The first Track race took place in Athens in 1896 and has featured at every Olympic Games but one since then. The Road Race also appeared in 1896 and was contested over an 87km course that began and ended in Athens. The cross-country Mountain Bike joined the roster in Atlanta 1996, before BMX completed the quartet in fast and frenetic style at Beijing 2008.

The lowdown

Track
Venue: Velodrome – Olympic Park

Dates: Thursday 2 – Tuesday 7 August

Medal events: 10

Road
Venue: The Mall (Road Race); Hampton Court Palace (Time Trial)

Dates: Saturday 28 July – Wednesday 1 August

Medal events: 4

Mountain Bike
Venue: Hadleigh Farm, Essex

Dates: Saturday 11 – Sunday 12 August

Medal events: 2

BMX
Venue: BMX Track – Olympic Park

Dates: Wednesday 8 – Friday 10 August

Medal events: 2

One to Watch

Julien Absalon (France)

A four-time Mountain Bike world champion with 17 World Cup wins, Absalon will be seeking a hat-trick of Olympic gold medals at London 2012, having taken the spoils at Athens 2004 and Beijing 2008.

Did you know?

The first Cycling Road Race in the Olympic Games in 1896 was a return trip from Athens to Marathon and a mere six riders took part.

Amazing fact!

Track bikes have no brakes. The riders stop themselves by applying pressure to their pedals instead.

British Track cyclists Bradley Wiggins (left) and Mark Cavendish compete in the Beijing 2008 Olympic Games.

What they say

'As a British athlete, as a British sportsman, the Olympics is the biggest thing.'

Great Britain's sprint king road racer Mark Cavendish.

Equestrian

The Equestrian events test the competitors' skill and ability but also their relationship with their horse...

Know the events

Equestrian consists of three disciplines: Dressage, where riders have to demonstrate their control over their horse, Jumping (or Show Jumping as it is sometimes called) and Eventing, where riders must compete in dressage, cross-country and jumping. In short, it is the complete test not just of riders' ability but of their relationship with their horse. There are six medal events, with Individual and Team honours to be won.

Olympic Games history

Equestrian events were included in the Olympic Games for the first time in 1900 and then in 1912, in a format not dissimilar to that used at Athens 2004. In the past, Eventing had been restricted to military officers, and while the Jumping and Dressage competitions were open to civilians, only a handful of civilian riders competed up to London 1948.

Britain's William Fox-Pitt in the Individual Eventing competition in Beijing 2008. He has high hopes of winning a medal at London 2012.

The lowdown

Dressage
Venue: Greenwich Park

Dates: Thursday 2 August – Thursday 9 August

Medal events: 2

Eventing
Venue: Greenwich Park

Dates: Saturday 28 July – Tuesday 31 July

Medal events: 2

Jumping
Venue: Greenwich Park

Dates: Saturday 4 – Wednesday 8 August

Medal events: 2

Sweden's Carl Gustaf Lewenhaupt won bronze in the Individual Jumping in 1920 and silver in the Team Eventing in Paris 1924.

Did you know?

The Equestrian events are the only ones in the Olympic Games in which men and women compete against each other on equal terms.

Amazing fact!

At the Helsinki 1952 and Melbourne/Stockholm 1956 Olympic Games Denmark's Lis Hartel won the silver medal in the Dressage event despite being paralysed below the knee.

What they say

'It's a pretty impossible feeling to describe. It's everything you would imagine it is. It's a huge honour to stand on the podium and see the flag go up.'

Gina Miles, USA Eventing silver medallist at Beijing 2008, on what it is like to win an Olympic medal.

One to watch

Hinrich Romeike (Germany)

He's a dentist by day but a double gold medal-winning Olympic champion when he's not doing root canal work. The winner of the Individial Eventing title at Beijing 2008, Romeike steered Germany to glory in the Team event too.

Gymnastics

Combining incredible strength and control with artistic poise, Gymnastics is one of the great spectacles of the Games...

Know the events

The Gymnastics programme at London 2012 is divided into three categories: Rhythmic, Artistic and Trampoline. The Rhythmic section is just one of two women-only sports in the Olympic Games and is a mixture of gymnastics and dance, with competitors performing floor exercises to music using a ball, clubs, a hoop and a ribbon. Artistic Gymnastics features Team and Individual events, with the men competing on the floor, pommel horse, rings, vault, parallel bars and horizontal bar, and the women performing on the vault, uneven bars, balance beam and floor. There are two events in the Trampoline.

Olympic Games history

The oldest of all Olympic Gymnastic disciplines is the Artistic programme, which appeared in the inaugural modern Olympic Games in Athens in 1896. The Rhythmic discipline didn't make its Olympic debut until the Los Angeles 1984 Olympic Games, with a new group event added at the Atlanta 1996 Games, while the Trampoline events are the newest inclusion, having made their Olympic debut at Sydney 2000.

The lowdown

Artistic Gymnastics
Venue: North Greenwich Arena

Dates: Saturday 28 July – Tuesday 7 August

Medal events: 14

Rhythmic Gymnastics
Venue: Wembley Arena

Dates: Thursday 9 – Sunday 12 August

Medal events: 2

Trampoline
Venue: North Greenwich Arena

Dates: Friday 3 – Saturday 4 August

Medal events: 2

Germany's Carl Schuhmann demonstrates incredible balance on the horse vault on the way to winning gold at the Athens 1896 Olympic Games.

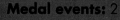

Did you know?

The word 'gymnastics' comes from the Greek word 'gymnos', which translates literally as 'naked'. Indeed, the male competitors in ancient Greece used to compete without any clothes, which is why women were banned from participating and spectating.

34

One to watch

Nastia Liukin (USA)

The only child of former Soviet gymnasts Valeri Liukin and Anna Kotchneva, Nastia Liukin is a four-time world champion and winner of the all-round Individual Olympic gold at Beijing 2008. having taken a year-long break, the Moscow-born 22-year-old is now planning to defend her title at London 2012.

What they say

'Everyone keeps telling me how old I am but the motivation is there, and the main motivation is London 2012.'

Great Britain's three-time world champion Beth Tweddle, 27, on what keeps her going.

Amazing fact!

The Russian-Ukrainian gymnast Larisa Latynina won 18 Olympic medals – the most ever won by a single athlete in any sport in Olympic history.

Football

The Olympic Football tournament will draw some of the greatest names in world football to London in 2012. Expect fireworks...

Know the event

With so many games to accommodate, the Football competition actually kicks off two days before the Olympic Games Opening Ceremony. As in previous Games, the men's tournament will be an under-23s event, although each country will be allowed to include three older players in their team. There are no age restrictions for the women's event. The format sees the best eight teams from the group stages qualifying for the quarter-finals and a knockout system culminating in the final game for the gold.

Olympic Games history

It will be 112 years since Football first featured in the Olympic Games when it kicks off at London 2012. Back in Paris 1900, it was Great Britain that took the gold medal and the sport has been played at every Games since, with the exception of Los Angeles in 1932. The reigning Olympic champions, Argentina, will not be defending their title at London 2012, as they failed to qualify. The women's tournament, meanwhile, will be staged for the fifth time at London 2012, having made its debut at Atlanta 1996.

The lowdown

Venue: City of Coventry Stadium (Coventry); Hampden Park (Glasgow); Millennium Stadium (Cardiff); Old Trafford (Manchester); St James' Park (Newcastle); Wembley Stadium

Dates: Wednesday 25 July – Saturday 11 August

Medal events: 2

Ones to watch

Japan

The Japanese women's team shocked the football world by taking the 2011 FIFA World Cup title in Germany, beating the much-fancied USA on penalties in the final. Certainly, they're going to be a force again at London 2012.

Did you know?

The only time a gold-medal match has been decided on penalties was in Sydney 2000, when Cameroon defeated Spain in a shootout.

Amazing fact!

Around 2,400 footballs will be used in the London 2012 Football competition.

What they say

'If I'm still playing and I'm still considered to make a difference to the team I'd love to be involved.'

Former England captain and London 2012 ambassador David Beckham.

Handball

Skill? Check. Speed? Check. Goals aplenty? You'd better believe it…

Know the event

Handball features two teams of seven players and is played on a court measuring 40 x 20 metres, the aim being to throw the ball into the opposition's goal. At London 2012, the format will see 12 teams split into two groups of six, with the best four teams in each group progressing to the knockout phase and the winners of the two semi-finals eventually competing for the gold medal.

Olympic Games history

The game of Handball, in its 11-man outdoor version, first appeared at the Olympic Games at Berlin 1936. It did not feature again until Munich 1972 when it became the seven-man indoor game we know today. Women's Handball, meanwhile, became an Olympic sport in 1976.

What they say

'It is a privilege for the young athletes to have the possibility to live the spirit and be part of these Olympic Games.'
French handball legend Jackson Richardson.

The lowdown

Venue: Copper Box – Olympic Park (preliminaries, women's quarter-finals); Basketball Arena – Olympic Park (men's quarter-finals, plus all semi-finals and finals)

Dates: Saturday 28 July – Sunday 12 August

Medal events: 2

Did you know?

Handball is said to be one of the oldest sports in existence, with evidence of the game in Homer's *Odyssey* and a third-century BC bronze statuette found in Dodoni, Greece.

Amazing fact!

If you think Handball sounds a bit like football but with the players using their hands instead of their feet, think again. Why? Because you're not going to get 50 goals in a 60-minute match of football.

Ones to watch

France

The success of the French national handball team – European champions, double world champions and reigning Olympic champions – has prompted a surge of interest in the game in France and led to commentators calling them the greatest handball team in history.

Rowing

There are few sports as gruelling and as strength-sapping as Olympic Rowing. Certainly, it takes a special kind of competitor to succeed...

Know the event

There will be 14 Olympic Rowing events at London 2012, ranging from the solo rowers in the Single Sculls right up to the Eights, which feature eight rowers plus a cox (the boat's navigator). Each race is over a 2,000m course and the competition begins with heats, from which the fastest boats will qualify for the next round. The competition continues until the final, where the medallists are decided.

Olympic Games history

The sport of Rowing has featured at every Olympic Games except the inaugural Games in Athens in 1896, when it was cancelled because of stormy seas. Up until the 1960s, it was the USA that largely dominated the events but gradually they were usurped by the Soviet Union and, thereafter, East Germany. Today, it is the unified Germany that perhaps offers the greatest strength in depth, although the sport's biggest ever star is Britain's Steve Redgrave, who won gold medals at no fewer than five Olympic Games.

The lowdown

Venue: Eton Dorney

Dates: Saturday 28 July – Saturday 4 August

Medal events: 14

Did you know?

Rowing is the only sport where competitors cross the finish line backwards.

What they say

'Self-belief is probably the most crucial factor in sporting success. The bodies are roughly equal, the training is similar, the techniques can be copied. What separates the achievers is nothing as tangible as split times or kilograms. It is the iron in the mind, not the supplements, that wins medals.'

Steve Redgrave, gold medal winner at five Olympic Games.

One to watch

Greg Searle (Great Britain)

It will be 20 years since Greg Searle won gold alongside his brother Jonny and their cox Gary Herbert at Barcelona 1992, but in 2010 he came out of retirement to race at the World Championships and now, aged 40, he's targeting another gold on home soil – or waters – at London 2012.

Amazing fact!

Dr Benjamin Spock, the world-renowned expert in child development, won Olympic gold in the men's Eights at the Paris 1924 Games.

Sailing

Feel the wind in your hair and the intense heat of Olympic competition in London 2012's Sailing events...

Know the event

There are 10 different Olympic Sailing events at London 2012 with six for men and four for women. Each event, irrespective of class, consists of a series of races and points are awarded according to the position each boat finishes, with one point for coming first, two for coming second and so on. In the final race – the medal race – the points are doubled, with the winner being the sailor or crew that has the fewest points.

Olympic Games history

Having made its Olympic debut in Paris 1900 (and then been omitted four years later in St Louis), Sailing has been almost ever-present at the Games. In recent years the team from Great Britain has led the way, topping the medal table at the last three Games. Can they make it four on their own waters?

What they say

'Not making the team in [Beijing] 2008 was really gutting. It affected me more than I thought and I realised how much I wanted it in 2012. It makes me more hungry this time around and competing at Weymouth will be incredibly exciting.'

Lucy Macgregor, British sailor.

Did you know?

Crown Prince Olav of Norway won gold in the Six-metre Sailing class at the Amsterdam 1928 Games.

The lowdown

Venue: Weymouth and Portland

Dates: Sunday 29 July – Saturday 11 August

Medal events: 10

Amazing fact!

The most successful Olympic sailor in Games history is Denmark's Paul Elvstrøm. He won gold medals at four consecutive Olympic Games, starting in 1948, and was still competing in 1988 at the age of 60.

One to watch

Ben Ainslie (Great Britain)

To win one gold medal is the ultimate achievement but to win three? Well, that just smacks of greed. However, it's what Britain's Ben Ainslie achieved at Sydney 2000, Athens 2004 and Beijing 2008. This, though, is possibly Ainslie's last Games and he's determined to end his Olympic journey in style.

Table Tennis

Fast, furious and frenetic, Olympic Table Tennis is the blink-and-you'll-miss-it sport that defies belief...

Know the event

Recent rule changes now mean that all Table Tennis Singles matches are played over the best of seven games, with the player reaching 11 points in each game the winner. In the Team event, the matches are made up of four singles matches and one doubles match, each played over the best of five games.

Olympic Games history

Table Tennis only joined the Olympic roster in 1988 and from day one it has been dominated by China. To date, the Chinese have won 20 of the 24 gold medals awarded and the only European to have taken a gold is the Swede Jan-Ove Waldner, who won the men's Singles at Barcelona in 1992.

The lowdown

Venue: ExCeL

Dates: Saturday 28 July – Wednesday 8 August

Medal events: 4

Did you know?

The game of table tennis was banned in the former Soviet Union during the early 20th century because the sport was believed to be harmful to the eyes.

Amazing fact!

Table tennis balls are made of super-lightweight celluloid and weigh just 2.7 grams.

What they say

'Train hard, improve your fitness, always fight and enjoy the sport! Take all criticism as potential advice – take on board the comments and then work hard to improve things!'

Paul Drinkhall, British number one ranked player.

One to watch

Wang Hao (China)

Wang Hao has his sights set on winning gold in the Singles event. At Beijing 2008, he missed out in the final, losing to his compatriot Ma Lin, but having regained his world number one ranking, he'll be desperate to go one better at London 2012.

Tennis

One of the great spectator sports, Tennis offers everything from subtlety and finesse to strategy and brute power…

Know the event

The Tennis competition at London 2012 will feature five medal events, each played on a knockout basis, with the semi-final winners playing off to win the gold. Like ATP Tour events, all matches will be the best of three sets, although the men's Singles final will be the best of five sets. The Mixed Doubles, making its first Olympic appearance since 1924, will be decided by a first to 10 points tie-break if the game stands at one set apiece.

Olympic Games history

Tennis may be a regular in the Olympic roster today but that has not always been the case. Although it appeared in the inaugural modern Olympic Games in Athens in 1896, it was omitted after Paris 1924 and didn't return until the Games in Seoul in 1988, when Miloslav Mecír (Czechoslovakia) and Steffi Graf (West Germany) won gold in the two Singles tournaments.

The lowdown

Venue: Wimbledon

Dates: Saturday 28 July – Sunday 5 August

Events: Men's and women's Singles and Doubles; Mixed Doubles

Medal events: 5

One to watch

Bernard Tomic (Australia)

While all the talk will doubtless be of Nadal, Djokovic and Federer, keep an eye out for the tenacious teenager from down under, Bernard Tomic. With the game and the confidence to match, he may just be the surprise package of London 2012's Tennis tournament.

Did you know?

The first tennis balls were made of wool or hair and wrapped up in leather while the first tennis rackets were wooden with strings made of sheep or cow's intestines.

Amazing fact!

Wimbledon also staged the Tennis when London first hosted the Olympic Games in 1908, with Great Britain winning all six gold medals.

What they say

'For me to be there in Beijing 2008, enjoying two weeks in the village with the rest of the sportsmen from around the world, but especially from Spain, was unforgettable.'

Spain's Rafa Nadal, Olympic Tennis champion at Beijing 2008.

Volleyball

There'll be bumping and blocking, setting and spiking galore at London 2012 as Volleyball and Beach Volleyball take centre stage...

Know the events

There are two types of Volleyball on offer at London 2012. The more traditional indoor Volleyball features teams of six players, while Beach Volleyball consists of just two players per side. At London 2012, Volleyball will begin with a preliminary phase with the 12 teams divided into two groups of six and where each team plays each other. The best eight teams then qualify for the knockout phase, with the winners of the semi-finals playing for the gold. Beach Volleyball will have a similar format and the 16, not eight, best teams qualify, although there will be 24 teams in the preliminaries, divided into six pools of four.

Olympic Games history

A comparatively new Olympic sport, Volleyball made its Olympic debut at the Tokyo1964 Games, where the gold medals were won by the Soviet Union (men) and Japan (women). Beach Volleyball didn't make its first appearance until Atlanta 1996 and the USA has dominated the event ever since, winning five of the eight Olympic gold medals awarded to date.

The lowdown

Volleyball
Venue: Earls Court

Dates: Saturday 28 July – Sunday 12 August

Medal events: 2

Beach Volleyball
Venue: Horse Guards Parade

Dates: Saturday 28 July – Thursday 9 August

Medal events: 2

What they say

'We hate to lose. What's great about Beach Volleyball is you can always find something to get better at. I don't think about losing. It could happen. I just go out there and play.'

Misty May-Treanor, America's double gold medal-winning Beach Volleyball star.

Did you know?

A five-a-side game with marked similarities to volleyball was actually played in the Middle Ages.

Ones to watch

Juliana Felisberta de Silva and Larissa Franca (Brazil)

Brazil's top duo, Felisberta and Franca, arrive at London 2012 as the new world champions, having defeated the two-time Olympic champions Misty May-Treanor and Kerri Walsh in the final. Can they repeat this success at London 2012?

Weightlifting

Superhuman feats of strength make Weightlifting one of the most engrossing sports at London 2012...

Know the event

The Weightlifting competition is divided into 15 different weight categories (eight for men, seven for women) with two types of lift – the snatch and the clean and jerk – in each class. In each of the formats, competitors are allowed three attempts to make a successful lift, with the weights of the good lifts counting towards their total. If there is a tie, the lifter with the lower body weight is declared the winner.

Olympic Games history

With the exception of the 1900, 1908 and 1912 Olympic Games, Weightlifting has always been part of the Olympic programme, although women began participating in Weightlifting only in the Sydney 2000 Games.

One to watch

Behdad Salimikordasiabi (Iran)

A national hero in Iran, Salimikordasiabi has become a formidable presence in the over 105kg Weightlifting class. A world title winner at his very first attempt in 2010, he also stunned the sport when a few months later he won the Asian Games by entering the action at 201kg in the snatch when everybody else was already out of the competition.

Wrestling

To be an Olympic Wrestling champion you need power and super-fast reflexes...

Know the event

Split into two styles – Greco-Roman and Freestyle — Wrestling is a combat sport where power, speed and technique are key. In the traditional Greco-Roman Wrestling, competitors are allowed to use only the arms and upper body to attack the upper body of their opponent, whereas in Freestyle Wrestling, they may use any part of their body as they try to wrestle their opponent to the ground.

Olympic Games history

Wrestling has appeared at every Olympic Games since 1896, with the exception of the Paris 1900. Freestyle Wrestling was first introduced at St Louis 1904, while Women's Wrestling made its Olympic debut at Athens 2004.

Did you know?

The longest Wrestling contest in Olympic history took place in the Stockholm 1912 Games when a middleweight bout between Finland's Alfred Asikainen and Russia's Martin Klein went on for an astonishing 11 hours!

The lowdown

Weightlifting
Venue: ExCeL

Dates: Saturday 28 July – Tuesday 7 August

Medal events: 15

Wrestling
Venue: ExCeL

Dates: Sunday 5 August – Sunday 12 August

Medal events: 18

43

Olympic Games athletes to watch

When London 2012 finally begins there'll be a wealth of world-class athletes on show...

Badminton

Lee Chong Wei

Country: Malaysia

A national hero in his native Malaysia, Lee Chong Wei took the silver medal in the men's Singles in the Beijing 2008 Olympic Games and was awarded the prestigious royal Datuk status for his many achievements in the sport. Expect him to go one better at London 2012.

Basketball

Kobe Bryant

Country: USA

Named the NBA's Player of the Decade in 2008, the Los Angeles Lakers shooting guard Kobe Bryant was a star of the USA team that took the gold at Beijing 2008. Indeed, he enjoyed the experience so much that he was one of first USA players to commit himself to the USA team for London 2012.

Modern Pentathlon

David Svoboda

Country: Czech Republic

Unquestionably, Svoboda is the form pentathlete of recent years and, as such, is one of the favourites when he competes. A European and world champion in recent years, he'll be desperate to add an Olympic title to his collection.

Hockey

Crista Cullen

Country: Great Britain

With a professional golfer father and a pro squash player for a mum, it was inevitable that Crista Cullen would inherit the sporting gene. Since making her international debut for England in 2003, the talented full-back has proved herself as one of the mainstays of the team, winning the 2006 Great Britain Hockey Athlete of the Year as well as Hockey Writers' Club Player of the Year.

Shooting

Niccolo Campriani
Country: Italy

The 24-year-old from Florence is the rising star of the 10m Air Rifle event and was actually the first athlete from any sport to qualify for London 2012 when he won the ISSF World Championship in Munich in August 2010.

Tennis

Petra Kvitová
Country: Czech Republic

Having taken her first Grand Slam title at Wimbledon in 2011, this dazzling young left-hander clearly loves playing at the famous venue and she'll be keen to maintain her winning streak there come London 2012.

Table Tennis

Wang Nan
Country: China

Having already won four Table Tennis gold medals in Sydney 2000, Athens 2004 and Beijing 2008, Wang Nan is hoping to secure another at London 2012 in the women's Singles. She won silver in the event in Beijing 2008, just missing out to compatriot Zhang Yining, and will be looking to win gold this summer.

Triathlon

Emma Snowsill
Country: Australia

The winner of the gold medal at Beijing 2008, Snowsill is another in the seemingly endless line of world-class Australian triathletes, having also won three World Championships and Commonwealth Games gold. She's looking to become the first triathlete to defend an Olympic title at London 2012.

Taekwondo

Jade Jones
Country: Great Britain

After her silver at the World Championships in Gyeongju, South Korea, in May 2011, this Youth Olympic Games gold medallist has now become a genuine gold medal hope in the -57kg division at London 2012.

Amazing facts!

Impress your friends and family with these fun London 2012 Games facts...

1 Over 200 countries will be sending competitors to the London 2012 Olympic and Paralympic Games, with more than 14,000 athletes taking part.

3 More than 5,250 people have worked on the construction of the new Olympic Stadium, with more than 240 businesses, from Devon up to Scotland, involved in the build.

2 The area of the Olympic Park in London's Lower Lee Valley is 2.5 sq km – or the same as 357 football pitches.

4 The London 2012 Velodrome has a roof made up of 17 km of steel cables, which when stretch out is twice the height of Mount Everest!

5 An estimated 260,000 loaves of bread are expected to be consumed at the London 2012 Olympic and Paralympic Games.

46

6

On the busiest day of the London 2012 Games, an estimated 800,000 people will use London's public transport system to travel to the Games.

7

The Opening and Closing Ceremonies of the London 2012 Games are expected to be watched by one in three of the world's population.

8

Competitors marched into the stadium for the first time in the Opening Ceremony at the London 1908 Games.

9

Since the modern Olympic Games began in 1896 a total of 12,513 medals have been awarded to competitors.

10

Before each Olympic Games, the Olympic Flame is lit at the ancient site of Olympia by capturing the sun's rays through a curved mirror. The Olympic Flame is then passed in a Torch Relay from Greece to the stadium of the host country.

Know the Paralympic Games sports

The Paralympic Games are the culmination of years of dedication, drive and sacrifice. Expect joy, tears and some truly superhuman performances…

Paralympic Archery

A keen eye, a steady arm and nerves of steel are required to succeed in the Paralympic Archery. At London 2012 the sport will take place at The Royal Artillery Barracks and there will be nine medal events across three classes: Standing (ST), Wheelchair 1 (W1) and Wheelchair 2 (W2).

Paralympic Cycling — Road

At London 2012, there will be 32 Paralympic Road Cycling events, with the Road Races and Time Trials supplemented by the Team Relay. There are four types of cycles used in these events: tandem, handcycle, tricycle and bicycle.

Paralympic Athletics

The largest sport at the Paralympic Games, Athletics will see 1,100 competitors giving their all in 170 medal events. Some athletes will compete in throwing frames or wheelchairs, some will have artificial limbs, while some visually impaired competitors will take part with the help of a sighted companion. All events will take place at the Olympic Stadium, apart from the road events, which will be starting at The Mall.

Paralympic Cycling — Track

Paralympic Cycling – Track is a test of speed, endurance and teamwork, and the sport will be one of highlights of the London 2012 Games. Consisting of 18 medal events (10 for men, seven for women and one mixed event), all of its races will take place at the Velodrome in the Olympic Park.

Boccia

Held at ExCel, Boccia is game of skill, nerve and tactics played on a rectangular court. At London 2012, there will be seven medal events on the programme in four different classes, all of which are open to athletes of either gender.

Paralympic Equestrian

There are 11 medal events for the 78 riders who will arrive in London for the Paralympic Games. There are three Dressage tests: a Team Test, an Individual Championship Test and a Freestyle Test, all of which are classified across five grades.

Football 5-a-side and 7-a-side

With two forms of the game at London 2012, Football fans will be in for a treat at the Paralympic Games. The 5-a-side format has just the one medal event for men, as does the 7-a-side version. The 5-a-side game is played by visually impaired athletes, using a ball with a noise making device, whereas the the 7-a-side variation is played by athletes with cerebral palsy. Other differences are the size of the pitch (it's bigger for 7-a-side) and the length of the games (5-a-side games last for 25 minutes each half and 7-a-side games for 30 minutes for each half).

Goalball

A perennially popular Paralympic sport, Goalball is played by visually impaired athletes using a ball with bells inside it. The aim of the game is to score in your opponents' goal by rolling the ball past their players. There are two medal events, one for the 12 men's teams and one for the 10 women's teams.

Powerlifting

Powerlifting is the ultimate test of upper-body strength and with 20 medals at stake – across 10 different weight categories for both men and women – you can be sure of some top-quality competition at London 2012. Here, athletes are grouped by body weight for competition, which means athletes with different impairments compete for the same medals.

Paralympic Judo

The athletes – or judoka – at London 2012 will all have visual impairments, which means, unlike in Olympic Judo, they are permitted to make contact with their opponent before the contest begins. There will be 13 medal events at the Paralympic Games.

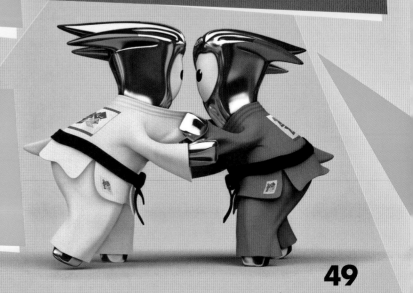

Paralympic Rowing

Making its second appearance in the Paralympic Games, the Rowing at London 2012 will feature four medal events, including two mixed-gender events – the Coxed Four and Double Sculls – plus the men's and women's Single Sculls. All the races will be held over a 1000m course on adapted rowing equipment.

Paralympic Sailing

Held in the picturesque setting of Weymouth and Portland, Paralympic Sailing has three mixed events: the Single-Person, Two-Person and Three-Person Keelboat competitions. All boats have open cockpits, requiring the crew to shift their weight from side to side to balance the boat.

Paralympic Swimming

One of only a handful of sports that has appeared at every Paralympic Games, Swimming remains among the largest events at London 2012, with 148 gold medals at stake. Athletes use four strokes at the Paralympic Games: Freestyle (or front crawl), Backstroke, Breaststroke and Butterfly.

Paralympic Table Tennis

An impressive 276 athletes will be competing in Table Tennis across 11 different classifications. Classes 1–5 cover wheelchair athletes, classes 6–10 cover standing athletes and class 11 covers athletes with intellectual disabilities.

Paralympic Shooting

Precision and skill are needed to make the grade in the Paralympic Shooting. The programme at London 2012 includes both rifle and pistol events, with three men's events, three women's events and six mixed events. There are also two classes of competition: SH1, for athletes who can support the weight of their firearm themselves, and SH2, for athletes who use a shooting stand to support their arm.

Volleyball — Sitting

With a 10-team men's competition and an eight-team women's competition, Sitting Volleyball, held at ExCeL, promises to be one of the most exciting events at the Paralympic Games. Fast and frenetic, it's a guaranteed crowd-pleaser.

Wheelchair Basketball

There's little or no difference between standard basketball and Wheelchair Basketball. The court is the same size, the basket is the same height from the ground and the scoring system is the same too. In short, it's every bit as gripping. Two medal events will be played at London 2012, with 12 men's teams and 10 women's teams taking part.

Wheelchair Fencing

You need your wits about you in Wheelchair Fencing. Competitors' wheelchairs are fixed to the ground to give them greater freedom of movement with their upper bodies and there are three types of weapon used: the Foil, the Epée and the Sabre. A total of 12 medals events are on offer.

Wheelchair Tennis

Wheelchair Tennis is virtually identical to Tennis, with the main difference being that the ball is allowed to bounce twice in Wheelchair Tennis, with only the first bounce needing to land in the court. At London 2012, there will be men's and women's Singles, men's and women's Doubles and Quad Singles and Quad Doubles, for players with an an impairment that affects three or more limbs.

Wheelchair Rugby

A mixed team sport (with just one event), Wheelchair Rugby is played on a full-size Basketball court with the aim of the game to cross your opponent's goal line. Competitors in Wheelchair Rugby must have a disability that affects both their arms and their legs.

Paralympic Athletics

To the Olympic Stadium where the Paralympic athetics records will be broken and memories made...

Know the event

With 1,100 athletes competing for 170 gold medals, Athletics is the biggest single sport at the Paralympic Games. There are different various strands to the Athletics competition, covering track events from 100m up to 5000m; field events (jumping and throwing) and the Marathon. Some athletes compete in wheelchairs or throwing frames, others with artificial limbs, and others with the assistance of a sighted companion.

Paralympic Games history

Athletics has been part of the Paralympic programme since the first official Games in Rome in 1960.

Did you know?

At Sydney 2000, USA track athlete Marla Runyan became the first visually impaired athlete to compete at the Olympic Games, finishing eighth in the 1500m final.

Monika Martina Willing of Germany competing in the Discus Throw final at the Beijing 2008 Paralympic Games.

Sweden's Monica Saker celebrates winning gold in the women's 800m race at the New York City/Stoke Mandeville 1984 Paralympic Games.

The lowdown

Venue: Olympic Stadium (track and field events); The Mall (road events)

Dates: Friday 31 August – Sunday 9 September 2012

Medal events: 170

One to watch

Oscar Pistorius (South Africa)

Nicknamed the 'Blade Runner', Oscar Pistorius was born with congenital absence of the fibula in both legs and now runs using carbon fibre artificial limbs. And boy does he run. A triple gold medal winner at Beijing 2008, he has already achieved the qualifying time in the 400m for the Olympic Games and now hopes to compete at both Games at London 2012.

Amazing fact!

'Hoopla' – a game based on the playground game, where rings are thrown on to a target pole – was actually an Athletics event at the original Stoke Mandeville Games.

List of events

- ✪ 100m
- ✪ 200m
- ✪ 400m
- ✪ 800m
- ✪ 1500m
- ✪ 5000m
- ✪ 4 x 100m Relay
- ✪ 4 x 400m Relay
- ✪ Club Throw
- ✪ Discus Throw
- ✪ High Jump
- ✪ Javelin Throw
- ✪ Long Jump
- ✪ Shot Put
- ✪ Triple Jump
- ✪ Marathon

Football 5-a-side and 7-a-side

There are two football formats at the Paralympic Games, but whichever one you watch you're guaranteed some world-class action...

Know the events

Taking place at the Riverbank Arena, 5-a-side Football is played by visually impaired competitors on a 42 x 22 metre pitch and, like Goalball, features a ball that makes sounds to help the players. 7-a-side Football, meanwhile, is for competitors with cerebral palsy and is played on a bigger pitch measuring no less than 70m x 50m and no more than 75m x 55m. While the games adhere to most FIFA rules, there is no offside in either format.

Paralympic Games history

The first international 7-a-side competiton took place in Edinburgh in 1978 at the Cerebral Palsy International Games. It was introduced in the New York and Stoke Mandeville Games in 1984, and has stayed on the Paralympic schedule ever since. The 5-a-side game first appeared at the Paralympic Games in Athens in 2004.

The lowdown

Football 5-a-side
Venue: Olympic Park – Riverbank Arena

Dates: Friday 31 August – Saturday 8 September 2012

Medal events: 1

Football 7-a-side
Venue: Olympic Park – Riverbank Arena

Dates: Saturday 1 September – Sunday 9 September 2012

Medal events: 1

Did you know?

All outfield players in the 5-a-side game are required to wear 'blackout' masks to ensure they compete on an equal basis.

Amazing fact!

Throw-ins may be made with only one hand.

One to watch

Michael Barker (Great Britain)

Michael Barker played with Wayne Rooney at the Everton Football Club Centre of Excellence before a road traffic accident cut short his blossoming career. Now acknowledged as one of the best cerebral palsy players in the world, Barker will be a key figure in the Great Britain team at London 2012.

Goalball

One of the most popular sports at the Paralympic Games is back again at London 2012 and it's going to be better than ever...

Know the event

Goalball is played by two teams of three visually impaired athletes on a court with tactile lines. The aim is to score by rolling the ball into the opposition's goal (9 x 1.3m high), while the opposition attempts to block the ball with their bodies. There are two medal events: a 12-team men's event and a 10-team women's event.

Paralympic Games history

Invented in 1946 for the rehabilitation of blind veterans after World War II, Goalball was introduced as a demonstration event at the Toronto 1976 Paralympic Games and then added to the Paralympic programme as a full medal sport four years later in Arnhem. The women's tournament first featured at the New York and Stoke Mandeville 1984 Games.

The lowdown

Venue: Olympic Park – Copper Box

Dates: Thursday 30 August – Friday 7 September 2012

Medal events: 2

The USA men's Goalball team take a shot against Germany at the Athens 2004 Games.

Did you know?

Goalball players all wear blackout masks on the court, which allows persons with varying degrees of vision to participate together.

Amazing fact!

There will be 150 sets of goggles used during the competition at London 2012.

What they say

'I would love to experience the atmosphere at the competition, which cannot be paralleled with any other experience in life. Also that it is in this country inspires me massively. There are so many world-class athletes who never get an opportunity to compete at their own Paralympics. What an honour!'

Great Britain's Michael Sharkey – brother of Anna!

One to watch

Anna Sharkey (Great Britain)

Anna first became interested in Goalball at a 'have-a-go' day, when she discovered she could play this team sport without being disadvantaged by her visual impairment. It's fair to say she found it to her liking. In 2009, she helped the Great Britain team to gold at the European Championships and as a 'Team 2012' athlete she is now being supported on her quest for success at the 2012 Games.

Paralympic Swimming

Water, water, every where – and a lot of gold medals to be won at the Aquatics Centre...

Know the event

There will be 600 swimmers competing in almost 150 medal events at the spectacular new Aquatics Centre, with four strokes – Freestyle, Backstroke, Breaststroke and Butterfly – being used in the competition. All races take place in the standard 50m pool but they may be started in a number of ways, including standing starts, sitting dives and from in the water as well. Swimmers are classified according to how their impairment affects their ability to perform each stroke.

Paralympic Games history

Swimming is one of the few sports to have featured at every Paralympic Games since they began in Rome in 1960.

The lowdown

Venue: Olympic Park – Aquatics Centre

Dates: Thursday 30 August – Saturday 8 September 2012

Medal events: 148

What they say

'I've got high expectations of myself. I'm quite a competitive person and I hate losing. Pressure drives me forward and makes me want to achieve so hopefully it will be like that for London 2012.'

Ellie Simmonds, Great Britain's double Paralympic Swimming champion from Beijing 2008.

Amazing fact!

'Tappers' are used to assist blind and visually impaired swimmers, who are tapped with a pole to tell them how long they have to go before they have to turn.

Did you know?

Blind swimmers are required to wear blackened goggles to ensure that competition is fair and equal.

One to watch

Natalie Du Toit (South Africa)

An international swimmer at the age of 14, Natalie Du Toit's swimming career looked to be in the balance after she was hit by a car in February 2001, an accident which resulted in her losing a leg. Within three months (and before she had learned to walk again) Natalie was back in the pool and her quest to become one of the greatest disabled athletes of all time was under way. A 10-time Paralympic gold medal winner, Natalie competes against able-bodied swimmers and made history by competing in both the Olympic and the Paralympic Games in Beijing in 2008.

Wheelchair Fencing

The exhilarating sport of Wheelchair Fencing requires precision, speed of thought and lightning-fast reflexes...

The lowdown

Venue: ExCeL

Dates: Tuesday 4 September – Saturday 8 September 2012

Medal events: 12

Know the event

There are three types of weapon used in Wheelchair Fencing. In bouts using the Foil and the heavier Epée, hits are scored by hitting an opponent with the tip of the weapon. In the Sabre, meanwhile, hits may also be scored with the edge of the weapon. The target area for the Foil is limited to the opponent's torso, while competitors in the Sabre and Epée events may be struck anywhere above the waist. There are 12 medal events at London 2012.

Paralympic Games history

Wheelchair Fencing was part of the very first Paralympic Games in Rome in 1960. At the Seoul Games in 1988, a new system of integrated classification was introduced, allowing athletes with different disabilities the opportunity to compete against each other

Did you know?

Fencing is competed at incredible speeds and in sport the only thing faster than the tip of a fencer's sword is a speeding bullet!

Amazing fact!

The distance between fencers at the start of a bout is decided by the fencer with the shorter arm. It is their decision whether to fence at their own distance, that of their opponent or anywhere between the two.

One to watch

Chui Yee Yu (Hong Kong)

Since she won gold on her first major appearance at the 2002 World Championships, Yu has continued to be the main threat in the Individual Foil and Epée events. At Athens 2004 she took gold in both events and managed to defend her Foil title in Beijing in 2008. She also won gold in Foil and Epée Team events at Athens 2004.

What they say

'On one side, it is very important that one is diligent and talented [as] success needs both of them. On the other side, only if one works a lot with endurance can one turn that diligence and talents to results.'

Pál Szekeres, Hungary's celebrated Paralympian and wheelchair fencer.

Paralympic Games athletes to watch

Look out for these Paralympic superstars at London 2012 this summer...

Boccia

Karen Kwok

Country: Hong Kong

Kwok sprang into the spotlight at Beijing 2008 when she beat the favourite, Nigel Murray of Great Britain, to land the Individual BC2 Boccia gold at the National Convention Center.

Equestrian

Lee Pearson

Country: Great Britain

In his three Paralympic Games in Sydney 2000, Athens 2004 and Beijing 2008, Pearson has won an impressive nine gold medals, taking the title in Individual Championship Test, Freestyle Test and Team Test. In 2009, he was made a Commander of the British Empire for his achievements.

Rowing

Tom Aggar

Country: Great Britain

Former rugby player Aggar turned to Rowing after suffering spinal injuries in an accident in 2005 and his success in the sport ever since has been truly startling. A gold medal winner at Beijing 2008, he recently won his fourth World Championship title too.

Powerlifting

Siamand Rahman

Country: Iran

In a country where powerlifters are feted like A-list celebrities, Siamand Rahman is verging on God-like status. At the 2010 Asian Para Games in Guangzhou, China, he smashed the world record in the +100kg category with a lift of 290kg, despite still being eligible for the junior competition. Expect big things of him in his first Paralympic Games at London 2012.

Sailing

Alexandra Rickham and Niki Birrell

Country: Great Britain

Rickham and Birrell have high hopes of success at the Paralympic Games. At the recent IFDS World Championship (held at the London 2012 Sailing venue in Weymouth and Portland) the pair dominated proceedings, wrapping up their third world title in the Skud-18 class. 'We just want to win the Games now,' says Birrell.

Shooting

Jonas Jacobsson

Country: Sweden

Where do you begin with someone like Jonas Jacobsson? Not only has he competed in every Paralympic Games since 1980 but he also shows no sign of losing any of his form, with his three gold medals at Beijing 2008 taking his medal tally to 25 (including 16 gold medals.)

Wheelchair Basketball

Country: USA

The reigning Paralympic and world champions, the USA women's Wheelchair Basketball are the team to watch at London 2012, and the fact that their closest rivals are their neighbours from the north, Canada, makes the prospect of another clash in London even more enticing.

Table Tennis

Natalia Partyka

Country: Poland

A Singles gold medal winner at Athens 2004 and Beijing 2008, Natalia Partyka also holds the distinction of being one of only two athletes – the other being the swimmer Natalie Du Toit – who have competed in both the 2008 Olympic and the Paralympic Games.

Volleyball – Sitting

Country: Iran

The men's Iranian Sitting Volleyball team showed just how resilient and determined they are when, having lost out to Bosnia-Herzegovina in the final at Athens 2004, they returned to take gold at Beijing 2008. Don't bet against them at London 2012.

Wheelchair Tennis

Aniek Van Koot

Country: The Netherlands

While the overwhelming favourite for the women's Singles gold will be the legendary Esther Vergeer, try and keep an eye out for her compatriot Aniek Van Koot, who at just 21 is already ranked fourth in the world and is the youngest player in the top 10.

London 2012 in numbers

As the biggest sporting event in the world, it's hardly surprising that the London 2012 Olympic Games and Paralympic Games are packed full of facts, figures and fun...

503

The number of different events taking place in the 20 sports of the London 2012 Paralympic Games.

80,000

The capacity of the new London 2012 Olympic Stadium in Stratford.

3,500

The cost in pounds of each of the specially designed titanium chairs that the Wheelchair Basketball players will use at London 2012.

10.8

The total number of tickets, in millions, available to spectators for the London 2012 Olympic and Paralympic Games.

17,320

The number of beds available for athletes in the London 2012 Olympic Village. Each competitor will have 16msq of floor space.

17,500

The number of spectators who can be accommodated at the new London 2012 Aquatics Centre, which will host the Swimming, Paralympic Swimming, Diving, Synchronised Swimming and the swimming element of the Modern Pentathlon.

26

The total number of different sports that will feature in the London 2012 Olympic Games.

350,000

The number of nails used by the team of 26 carpenters in installing the Siberian Pine track at the new London 2012 Velodrome.

8,000

The number of people who will carry the Olympic Torch on its 70-day journey from Greece to London.

London 2012 Olympic Games competition schedule

Sport	Venue	25 Wed	26 Thurs	27 Fri	28 Sat	29 Sun	30 Mon	31 Tues	1 Wed	2 Thurs	3 Fri	4 Sat	5 Sun	6 Mon	7 Tues	8 Wed	9 Thurs	10 Fri	11 Sat	12 Sun
Opening Ceremony	Olympic Park – Olympic Stadium			●																
Archery	Lord's Cricket Ground			●	●	●	●	●	●	●	●									
Athletics	Olympic Park – Olympic Stadium										●	●	●	●	●	●	●	●	●	●
Athletics – Marathon	The Mall												●							●
Athletics – Race Walk	The Mall											●							●	
Badminton	Wembley Arena				●	●	●	●	●	●	●	●	●							
Basketball	Olympic Park – White Hall				●	●	●	●	●	●	●	●	●	●	●					
	North Greenwich Arena															●	●	●	●	●
Beach Volleyball	Horse Guards Parade				●	●	●	●	●	●	●	●	●	●	●	●	●			
Boxing	ExCeL				●	●	●	●	●	●	●	●	●	●	●	●	●	●	●	●
Canoe Slalom	Lee Valley White Water Centre					●	●	●	●	●										
Canoe Sprint	Eton Dorney													●	●	●	●	●	●	
Cycling – BMX	Olympic Park – BMX Track															●	●	●		
Cycling – Mountain Bike	Hadleigh Farm, Essex																		●	●
Cycling – Road	The Mall				●	●														
	Hampton Court Palace								●											
Cycling – Track	Olympic Park – Velodrome									●	●	●	●	●	●					
Diving	Olympic Park – Aquatics Centre					●	●	●	●		●	●	●	●	●	●	●	●	●	
Equestrian – Dressage	Greenwich Park									●	●				●		●			
Equestrian – Eventing	Greenwich Park				●	●	●	●												
Equestrian – Jumping	Greenwich Park											●	●	●						
Fencing	ExCeL				●	●	●	●	●	●	●	●	●							
Football	City of Coventry Stadium, Coventry	●	●		●	●		●	●		●						●			
	Hampden Park, Glasgow	●	●		●				●		●									
	Millennium Stadium, Cardiff	●	●		●				●		●	●						●		
	Old Trafford, Manchester		●				●				●			●	●					
	St James' Park, Newcastle		●				●				●									
	Wembley Stadium					●			●			●			●	●		●	●	
Gymnastics – Artistic	North Greenwich Arena				●	●	●	●	●					●	●					
Gymnastics – Rhythmic	Wembley Arena																●	●	●	●
Gymnastics – Trampoline	North Greenwich Arena										●	●								
Handball	Olympic Park – Copper Box				●	●	●	●	●	●	●	●	●	●	●					
	Olympic Park – White Hall															●	●	●	●	
Hockey	Olympic Park – Riverbank Arena					●	●	●	●	●	●	●	●	●	●	●	●	●	●	
Judo	ExCeL				●	●	●	●	●	●	●									
Modern Pentathlon	Olympic Park and Greenwich Park																		●	●
Rowing	Eton Dorney, Buckinghamshire				●	●	●	●	●	●	●	●								
Sailing	Weymouth and Portland, Dorset					●	●	●	●	●	●	●	●	●	●	●	●	●	●	
Shooting	The Royal Artillery Barracks				●	●	●	●	●	●	●	●	●							
Swimming	Olympic Park – Aquatics Centre				●	●	●	●	●	●	●	●								
Swimming – Marathon	Hyde Park																●	●		
Synchronised Swimming	Olympic Park – Aquatics Centre												●	●	●		●	●		
Table Tennis	ExCeL				●	●	●	●	●	●	●	●	●	●		●				
Taekwondo	ExCeL															●	●	●	●	
Tennis	Wimbledon				●	●	●	●	●	●	●	●	●							
Triathlon	Hyde Park											●			●					
Volleyball	Earls Court				●	●	●	●	●	●	●	●	●	●	●	●	●	●	●	●
Water Polo	Olympic Park – Water Polo Arena					●	●	●	●	●	●	●	●	●	●	●	●	●	●	●
Weightlifting	ExCeL				●	●	●	●	●			●	●	●	●	●				
Wrestling – Freestyle	ExCeL																	●	●	●
Wrestling – Greco-Roman	ExCeL													●	●	●				
Closing Ceremony	Olympic Park – Olympic Stadium																			●